| designed by Margret Willson

ABBREVIATIONS

rep	repeat
rnd(s)	round(s)
RS	right side
sk	skip
sp(s)	space(s)
st(s)	stitch(es)
WS	wrong side

SPECIAL TERMS

dc2tog: Double crochet 2 together—[Yarn over, insert hook in next st and draw up a loop, yarn over and draw through 2 loops] twice, yarn over and draw through all 3 loops on hook.

dc3tog: Double crochet 3 together—[Yarn over, insert hook in next st and draw up a loop, yarn over and draw through 2 loops] 3 times, yarn over and draw through all 4 loops on hook.

sc2tog: Single crochet 2 together—Insert hook in next st, yarn over and draw up a loop, (2 loops on hook), insert hook in next st, yarn over and draw up a loop, yarn over and draw through all 3 loops on hook.

STITCHES USED

Chain (ch)
Double crochet (dc)
Half double crochet (hdc)
Single crochet (sc)
Slip stitch (sl st)

Stitch Pattern

(over any number of sts)
Row 1 (WS): Ch 1, sc in each dc across, turn.

Row 2 (RS): Ch 3 (counts as dc here and throughout), dc in each sc across, turn.
Rep Rows 1 and 2 for Stitch Pattern.

STRIPE SEQUENCE

*Work 1 row with B, 1 row with C, 1 row with D, 1 row with A, 1 row with E; rep from * as needed.

NOTE

To change color, work last st of old color to last yarn over. Yarn over with new color and draw through all loops on hook to complete st. Continue working with new color.

BACK

With B, ch 59 (63, 65, 69).

Row 1 (RS): Dc in 3rd ch from hook (beginning ch does not count as a st) and in each ch across, turn—57 (61, 63, 67) dc. Change to C.

Rows 2–14: Continue to change color as in Stripe Sequence and, beginning with Row 1 of Stitch Pattern, rep Rows 1 and 2 of Stitch Pattern for a total of 14 rows. **Note:** You should end with a WS row (Row 1 of Stitch Pattern), worked with A. Do not change color at the end of the last row.

Working with A only, continue repeating Rows 1 and 2 of Stitch Pattern until piece measures 6$\frac{1}{2}$ (7, 7$\frac{1}{2}$, 7$\frac{1}{2}$)"/16.5 (18, 19,19) cm from beginning; end with a WS row.

sophisticated
baby & toddler

NaturallyCaron.com Spa yarn is a silky bamboo blend that you must touch to believe. It's also washable, making it perfect for crocheting soft afghans and garments for wee folk! Use Spa to create these darling designs for babies and toddlers. There are two blankets and a vest, as well as two colorful tops for girls. There's also a handy bag for a busy mom. It has an easy-access flap closure and adjustable shoulder strap— just right for carrying Baby's necessities.

Leisure Arts, INC.
Little Rock, Arkansas

flower child
sweater

 **EASY**

SIZES: 1 (2, 3, 4) years

FINISHED MEASUREMENTS
Chest 23 (24, 25, 27)"/58.5 (61, 63.5, 68.5)cm
Length 11 (12, 12$^1/_2$, 13)"/28 (30.5, 32, 33)cm

MATERIALS
Caron International's Naturally Caron Spa
(75% microdenier acrylic, 25% rayon from bamboo;
3 oz/85g, 251 yds/230m):
#0004 Green Sheen, 6 (6, 9, 9) oz (A)
#0005 Ocean Spray, 3 oz (B)
#0002 Coral Lipstick, 3 oz (C)
#0003 Soft Sunshine, 3 oz (D)
#0001 Rose Bisque, 3 oz (E)

Crochet hook, size US G/6 (4mm), or size to obtain gauge
Yarn needle

GAUGE
In Stitch Pattern, 20 sts = 4"/10cm and 14 rows = 3$^3/_4$"/9.5cm

Instructions continued on page 4.

Shape Armholes

Row 1 (RS): Ch 1, sl st across first 5 (5, 5, 6) sts, ch 2 (does not count as a st), dc in next 46 (50, 52, 54) sts, dc2tog, turn; leave remaining sts unworked—47 (51, 53, 55) dc.

Row 2: Ch 1, sc2tog, sc in each dc across to last 2 dc, sc2tog, turn—45 (49, 51, 53) sc.

Row 3: Ch 2, sk first st, dc in each sc across to last 2 sc, dc2tog, turn—43 (47, 49, 51) dc.

Beginning with Row 1 of Stitch Pattern, rep Rows 1 and 2 of Stitch Pattern until armhole measures 4 (4$\frac{1}{2}$, 4$\frac{1}{2}$, 5)"/10 (11.5, 11.5, 12.5) cm; end with a WS row.

Shape First Shoulder

Row 1 (RS): Ch 1, sc in next 3 (3, 3, 4) sts, hdc in next 3 (4, 4, 4) sts, dc in next 4 (5, 5, 5) sts; leave remaining sts unworked—10 (12, 12, 13) sts. Fasten off.

Shape Second Shoulder

Row 1 (RS): Sk 23 (23, 25, 25) unworked sts following first shoulder, join yarn in next st, ch 3 (counts as dc), dc in next 3 (4, 4, 4) sts, hdc in next 3 (4, 4, 4) sts, sc in next 3 (3, 3, 4) sts—10 (12, 12, 13) sts. Fasten off.

FRONT

Work as for back until armhole measures 3 (3$\frac{1}{2}$, 3$\frac{1}{2}$, 4)"/ 7.5 (9, 9, 10) cm from beginning of armhole shaping; end with a WS row—43 (47, 49, 51) sts.

Shape First Shoulder and Neck

Row 1 (RS): Ch 3, dc in next 10 (12, 12, 13) sts, dc2tog, turn; leave remaining sts unworked—12 (14, 14, 15) sts.

Row 2: Ch 1, sc2tog, sc in each st across, turn—11 (13, 13, 14) sts.

Row 3: Ch 3, dc in next 8 (10, 10, 11) sts, dc2tog, turn—10 (12, 12, 13) sts.

Row 4: Ch 1, sc in each st across, turn.

Row 5: Ch 1, sc in next 3 (3, 3, 4) sts, hdc in next 3 (4, 4, 4) sts, dc in next 4 (5, 5, 5) sts. Fasten off.

Shape Second Shoulder and Neck

Row 1 (RS): Sk 17 (17, 19, 19) unworked sts following first shoulder, join A in next st, ch 2 (does not count as a st), dc in each remaining st across, turn—12 (14, 14, 15) sts.

Row 2: Ch 1, sc in next 10 (12, 12, 13) sts, sc2tog, turn—11 (13, 13, 14) sts.

Row 3: Ch 2 (does not count as a st), sk first st, dc in each st across, turn—10 (12, 12, 13) sts.

Row 4: Ch 1, sc in each st across, turn.

Row 5: Ch 3, dc in next 3 (4, 4, 4) sts, hdc in next 3 (4, 4, 4) sts, sc in next 3 (3, 3, 4) sts. Fasten off.

Instructions continued on page 6.

SLEEVE (make 2)
With B, ch 33 (35, 35, 37).

Row 1 (RS): Dc in 3rd ch from hook (beginning ch does not count as a st) and in each ch across, turn— 31 (33, 33, 35) dc. Change to C.

Row 2 (WS): Ch 1, sc in each dc across, turn. Change to D.

Row 3 (increase row): Ch 3, dc in first sc (increase made), dc in each sc across to last sc, 2 dc in last sc, turn—33 (35, 35, 37) dc. Change to A.

Note: In the following rows, continue to change color as in Stripe Sequence for a total of 14 rows. Then change to A, and work all remaining rows of sleeve with A only.

Rows 4–6: Beginning with Row 1 of Stitch Pattern, work 3 rows in Stitch Pattern.

Rows 7–30: Rep Rows 3–6 six more times—45 (47, 47, 49) sts.

Beginning with Row 2 of Stitch Pattern, work even in Stitch Pattern until piece measures 8 (8$\frac{1}{2}$, 9$\frac{1}{2}$, 10$\frac{1}{2}$)"/20.5 (21.5, 24, 26.5) cm; end with a WS row.

Shape Cap

Row 1 (RS): Sl st in first 5 (5, 5, 6), ch 2 (does not count as st), dc in next 34 (36, 36, 36) sts, dc2tog, turn; leave remaining sts unworked— 35 (37, 37, 37) sts.

Row 2: Ch 1, sc2tog, sc in each dc to last 2 dc, sc2tog, turn— 33 (35, 35, 35) sts.

Row 3: Ch 2, sk first st, dc in each sc to last 2 sc, dc2tog, turn— 31 (33, 33, 33) sts.

Row 4: Ch 1, sc2tog, sc in each dc to last 2 dc, sc2tog, turn— 29 (31, 31, 31) sts.

Rows 5–6 (8, 8, 10): Rep last 2 rows 1 (2, 2, 3) more times— 25 (23, 23, 19) sts.

Row 7 (9, 9, 11): Ch 2, sk first st, dc2tog, dc in each st across to last 3 sts, dc3tog—21 (19, 19, 15) sts. Fasten off.

FLOWER (make 3 – 1 each with C, D, and E)
Ch 6; join with sl st in first ch to form a ring.

Rnd 1: [2 sc in ring, ch 3, sc in ring] 5 times; join with sl st in first sc— 15 sc, and 5 ch-3 sps.

Rnd 2: *Sk next sc, 9 dc in next ch-3 sp, sk next sc, sl st in next sc; rep from * around; working last sl st in joining sl st of Rnd 1. Fasten off.

FINISHING

Sew shoulder seams. Set in sleeves. Sew side and sleeve seams.

Neckband

With RS facing, join B in shoulder seam,

Rnd 1 (RS): Ch 1, work 68 (68, 72, 72) sc evenly around neck edge; join with sl st in first sc, turn.

Rnd 2 (WS): Ch 1, sc in first 2 sc, (sc, ch 3, sc) in next sc, *sc in next 3 sc, (sc, ch 3, sc) in next sc; rep from * around to last sc, sc in last sc; join with sl st in first sc, do not turn.

Rnd 3: *Sk next sc, 9 dc in next ch-3 sp, sk next sc, sl st in next sc; rep from * around, working last sl st in joining sl st of previous rnd. Fasten off leaving a long tail for sewing.

Thread tail onto yarn needle, fold neckband to right side and working through back loops of Rnd 3 only, tack in place around neck.

With yarn needle and yarn to match flower, sew flowers to front of sweater. Sew through back loops only and use photograph as a guide.

Using yarn needle, weave in all ends.

flower child sweater schematic

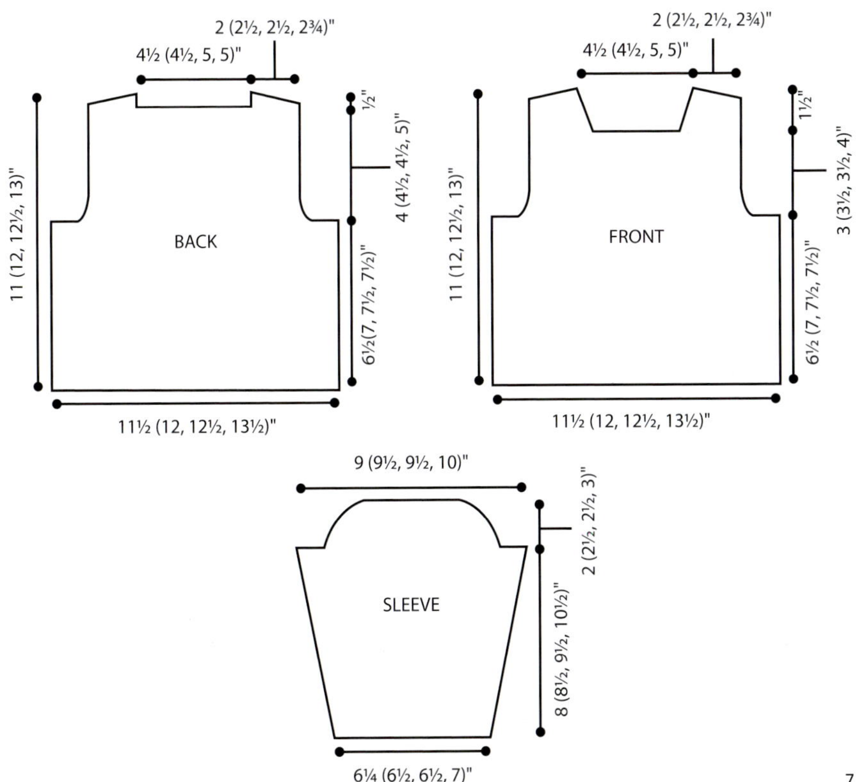

cabled baby
vest

SIZES: 9 months (12 months, 18 months, 2 years, 3 years)

FINISHED MEASUREMENTS

Chest 20 (21$^{1}/_{2}$, 22$^{1}/_{2}$, 24, 25$^{1}/_{2}$)"/51 (54.5, 57, 61, 65)cm
Length 13 (14, 14, 15, 15)"/33 (35.5, 35.5, 38, 38)cm, not including
hood

MATERIALS

Caron International's Naturally Caron Spa
(75% microdenier acrylic, 25% rayon from bamboo;
3 oz/85g, 251 yds/230m):
#0006 Berry Frappe 8 (8, 8, 8, 8) oz

Crochet hook, size US H/8 (5mm), or size to obtain gauge
Stitch markers
Yarn needle
4 (4, 5, 5, 5) toggle-style shank buttons, 1$^{1}/_{4}$"/32mm long
Sewing needle and matching thread

GAUGE

In pattern, 12 sts and 7 rows = 4"/10cm

Instructions continued on page 10.

| designed by Reneé Barnes

ABBREVIATIONS

rep	repeat
RS	right side
sk	skip
st(s)	stitch(es)
WS	wrong side

SPECIAL TERMS

FPdc: Front-post double crochet—
Yarn over, insert hook from front to
back and then to front again around
post of st, yarn over and draw up
loop, [yarn over and draw through
2 loops on hook] twice.

BPdc: Back-post double crochet—
Yarn over, insert hook from back to
front and then to back again around
post of st, yarn over and draw up
loop, [yarn over and draw through
2 loops on hook] twice.

FPtr: Front-post treble crochet—
[Yarn over] twice, insert hook from
front to back and then to front again
around post of st, yarn over and
draw up a loop, [yarn over and draw
through 2 loops on hook] 3 times.

2/2 Right Cross: Sk next 2 sts, FPtr
around next 2 sts, working behind sts
just worked, FPtr around 2 skipped
sts.

2/2 Left Cross: Sk next 2 sts, FPtr
around next 2 sts, working in front
of sts just worked, FPtr around 2
skipped sts.

1/1 Right Cross: Sk next st, FPtr
around next st, working behind st
just worked, FPtr around skipped st.

1/1 Left Cross: Sk next st, FPtr
around next st, working in front of st
just worked, FPtr around skipped st.

STITCHES USED

Chain (ch)
Double crochet (dc)
Single crochet (sc)
Slip stitch (sl st)

NOTE

Vest is worked holding 2 strands of
yarn together throughout, unless
otherwise stated. To make it easier to
work with two strands of yarn held
together, consider purchasing
4 skeins of yarn, or roll the skeins into
4 separate balls before beginning.

BODY

With 2 strands of yarn held together,
ch 62 (66, 70, 74, 78).

Row 1 (RS): Dc in 4th ch from hook
(beginning ch counts as first dc) and
in each ch across, turn—
60 (64, 68, 72, 76) dc.

Row 2: Ch 3 (counts as first dc
here and throughout), dc in next
2 (3, 4, 5, 6) dc, BPdc around next
4 sts, dc in next 3 dc, BPdc around
next 2 sts, dc in next 6 (7, 8, 9, 10) dc,
BPdc around next 4 sts, dc in next
4 dc, BPdc around next 8 sts, dc in
next 4 dc, BPdc around next 4 sts,
dc in next 6 (7, 8, 9, 10) dc, BPdc
around next 2 sts, dc in next 3 dc,
BPdc around next 4 sts, dc in next
3 (4, 5, 6, 7) dc, turn.

Row 3: Ch 3, dc in next 2 (3, 4, 5, 6)
dc, FPdc around next 4 sts, dc in next
3 dc, FPdc around next 2 sts, dc in
next 6 (7, 8, 9, 10) dc, FPdc around
next 4 sts, dc in next 4 dc, FPdc
around next 8 sts, dc in next 4 dc,

FPdc around next 4 sts, dc in next 6 (7, 8, 9, 10) dc, FPdc around next 2 sts, dc in next 3 dc, FPdc around next 4 sts, dc in next 3 (4, 5, 6, 7) dc, turn.

Row 4: Rep Row 2.

Row 5: Ch 3, dc in next 2 (3, 4, 5, 6) dc, 2/2 Right Cross over next 4 sts, dc in next 3 dc, 1/1 Right Cross over next 2 sts, dc in next 6 (7, 8, 9, 10) dc, 2/2 Right Cross over next 4 sts, dc in next 4 dc, 2/2 Right Cross over next 4 sts, 2/2 Left Cross over next 4 sts, dc in next 4 dc, 2/2 Left Cross over next 4 sts, dc in next 6 (7, 8, 9, 10) dc, 1/1 Left Cross over next 2 sts, dc in next 3 dc, 2/2 Left Cross over next 4 sts, dc in next 3 (4, 5, 6, 7) dc, turn.

Rows 6–17: Rep Rows 2–5 three more times.

Place st markers in the 15th (16th, 17th, 18th, 19th) and 46th (49th, 52nd, 55th, 58th) sts of the last row. Do not fasten off.

LEFT FRONT

Row 18 (WS): Ch 3, dc in next 2 (3, 4, 5, 6) dc, BPdc around next 4 sts, dc in next 3 dc, BPdc around next 2 sts, dc in next 3 dc, turn.
Note: You will work the last st of Row 18 into the first marked dc. Leave the remaining sts unworked for back and right front (to be worked later)—15 (16, 17, 18, 19) sts.

Row 19: Ch 3, dc in next 2 dc, FPdc around next 2 sts, dc in next 3 dc, FPdc around next 4 sts, dc in next 3 (4, 5, 6, 7) dc, turn.

Row 20: Rep Row 18.

Row 21: Ch 3, dc in next 2 dc, 1/1 Left Cross, dc in next 3 dc, 2/2 Left Cross, dc in last 3 (4, 5, 6, 7) dc, turn.

Rows 22 and 23: Rep Rows 18 and 19.

Sizes 12 months (18 months, 2 years, 3 years) only: Rep Rows 20–21 (21, 22, 22).

All sizes: Fasten off.

RIGHT FRONT
With WS facing and 2 strands of yarn held together, join yarn with sl st in next marked dc of body.

Row 18: Ch 3, dc in next 2 dc, BPdc around next 2 sts, dc in next 3 dc, BPdc around next 4 sts, dc in last 3 (4, 5, 6, 7) dc, turn—15 (16, 17, 18, 19) sts.

Row 19: Ch 3, dc in next 2 (3, 4, 5, 6) dc, FPdc around next 4 sts, dc in next 3 dc, FPdc around next 2 sts, dc in last 3 dc, turn.

Row 20: Rep Row 18.

Row 21: Ch 3, dc in next 2 (3, 4, 5, 6) dc, 2/2 Right Cross, dc in next 3 dc, 1/1 Right Cross, dc in last 3 dc, turn.

Rows 22 and 23: Rep Rows 18 and 19.

Sizes 12 months (18 months, 2 years, 3 years) only: Rep Rows 20–21 (21, 22, 22).

All sizes: Fasten off.

Instructions continued on page 12.

BACK

With WS facing and 2 strands of yarn held together, sk the next 2 unworked sts following the left front (for armhole), join yarn with sl st in next st.

Row 18: Ch 3, dc in next 0 (1, 2, 3, 4) dc, BPdc around next 4 sts, dc in next 4 dc, BPdc around next 8 sts, dc in next 4 dc, BPdc around next 4 sts, dc in last 1 (2, 3, 4, 5) dc, turn.
Note: After the last st of Row 18 is worked, 2 unworked sts remain between the back and right front (for armhole)—26 (28, 30, 32, 34) sts.

Row 19: Ch 3, dc in next 0 (1, 2, 3, 4) dc, FPdc around next 4 sts, dc in next 4 dc, FPdc around next 8 sts, dc in next 4 dc, FPdc around next 4 sts, dc in last 1 (2, 3, 4, 5) dc, turn.

Row 20: Rep Row 18.

Row 21: Ch 3, dc in next 0 (1, 2, 3, 4) dc, 2/2 Right Cross, dc in next 4 dc, 2/2 Right Cross, 2/2 Left Cross, dc in next 4 dc, 2/2 Left Cross, dc in next 1 (2, 3, 4, 5) dc, turn.

Rows 22 and 23: Rep Rows 18 and 19.

Sizes 12 months (18 months, 2 years, 3 years) only: Rep Rows 20–21 (21, 22, 22).

All sizes: Fasten off.

HOOD

With 2 strands of yarn held together, ch 20 (24, 26, 28, 30).

Row 1 (RS): Dc in 4th ch from hook and in each ch across, turn— 18 (22, 24, 26, 28) dc.

Row 2: Ch 3, BPdc around next 4 dc, dc in last 13 (17, 19, 21, 23) dc, turn.

Row 3: Ch 3, dc in next 12 (16, 18, 20, 22) dc, FPdc around next 4 sts, dc in last dc, turn.

Row 4: Rep Row 2.

Row 5: Ch 3, dc in next 12 (16, 18, 20, 22) dc, 2/2 Left Cross, dc in last dc, turn.

Row 6: Rep Row 2.

Rows 7-30 (34, 34, 34, 38): Rep last 4 rows 6 (7, 7, 7, 8) more times.

Row 31 (35, 35, 35, 39): Rep Row 3. Fasten off.

Buttonband

Place 4 (4, 5, 5, 5) stitch markers evenly along front edge (right front for girls, left front for boys) for button loop placement. Place the first marker about 1/4"/6mm below neck edge, last marker about 3/4"/19mm above lower edge, and the remaining markers evenly spaced between the first and last. With RS facing and 2 strands of yarn together, join yarn with sc in corner of front edge, work sc evenly spaced across front edge, working ch 5 (for button loop) at each marker. Fasten off.

With RS together and one strand of yarn, begin at outer edge and sl st shoulders together for 1 (1¼, 1½, 1¾, 2)"/2.5 (3, 3.5, 4, 5)cm on each side.

Fold hood in half, bringing foundation ch to meet last row. Sew back edges together (front edge has cable). With RS together and one strand of yarn, sl st hood to neck of vest, easing to fit, and matching front edges and centers.

Vest Edging

With RS facing and 2 strands of yarn together, join yarn with sl st in center back of lower edge. Sc evenly around all edges of vest and front edge of hood, working 3 sc at each corner and working 5 sc in each ch-5 button loop; join with sl st in first sc. Fasten off.

Armhole Edging

With RS facing and 2 strands of yarn together, join yarn with sl st in underarm, sc evenly around armhole; join with sl st in first sc. Fasten off.

Sew buttons opposite button loops. Using yarn needle, weave in all ends.

cabled baby vest schematic

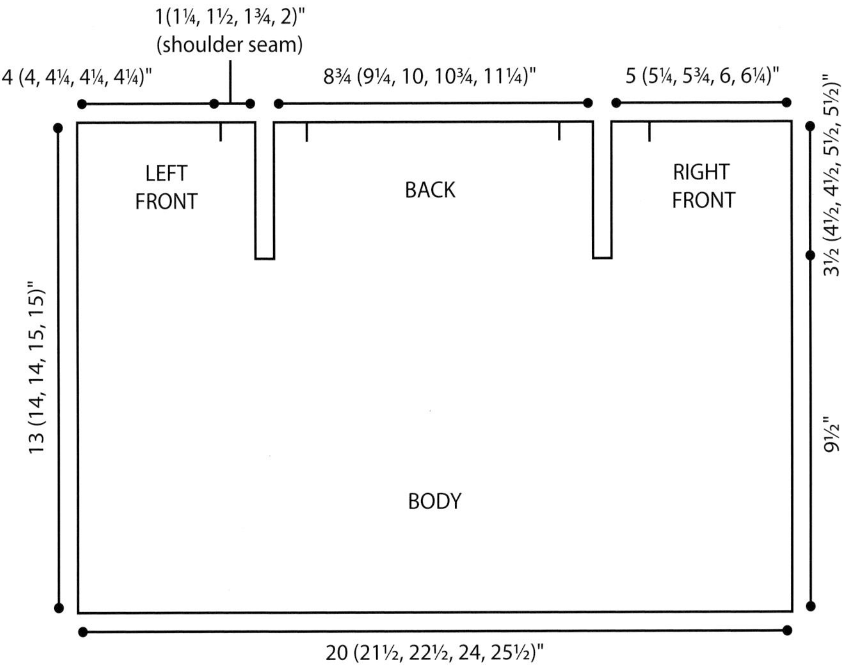

hippie girl
sweater

INTERMEDIATE

SIZES: 12 months (18 months, 2 years, 4 years, 5 years)

FINISHED MEASUREMENTS

Chest 21 (22, 24, 26, 27)"/53.5 (56, 61, 66, 68.5)cm
Length 13 (14$\frac{1}{2}$, 15$\frac{1}{2}$, 16$\frac{1}{2}$, 17$\frac{1}{2}$)"/33 (37, 39.5, 42, 44.5)cm

MATERIALS

Caron International's Naturally Caron Spa
(75% microdenier acrylic, 25% rayon from bamboo;
3 oz/85g, 251 yds/230m):
#0001 Rose Bisque 9 (9, 9, 12, 12) oz (A)
#0004 Green Sheen 3 oz (B)
#0007 Naturally 3 oz (C)

Crochet hooks, one each size US G/6 (4mm) and size US H/8 (5mm),
or sizes to obtain gauge
Stitch markers
Yarn needle

GAUGE

In double crochet, using US G/6 (4mm) hook, 17 sts and 11 rows =
4"/10cm;
In Seed Stitch pattern, using US H/8 (5mm) hook, 24 sts and 26 rows
= 4"/10cm.

Instructions continued on page 16.

| designed by Susan Shildmyer

rep	repeat
RS	right side
sk	skip
sp	space
st(s)	stitch(es)
WS	wrong side

SPECIAL TERMS

dc2tog: Double crochet 2 together—[Yarn over, insert hook in next st and draw up a loop, yarn over and draw through 2 loops] twice, yarn over and draw through all 3 loops on hook.

ldc: Long double crochet—Yarn over, insert hook in indicated st 2 rows below, yarn over and draw up a loop (to current row height), [yarn over and draw through two loops on hook] twice. **Note:** Do not work into the corresponding st in the current working row.

sc2tog: Single crochet 2 together—Insert hook in next st, yarn over and draw up a loop, (2 loops on hook), insert hook in next st, yarn over and draw up a loop, yarn over and draw through all 3 loops on hook.

STITCHES USED

Chain (ch)
Double crochet (dc)
Half double crochet (hdc)
Single crochet (sc)
Slip stitch (sl st)

Seed Stitch (over an even number of sts)
Row 1: Ch 1, sc in first sc, sc in next ch-1 sp, *ch 1, sk next sc, sc in next ch-1 sp; rep from * across to last 2 sc, ch 1, sk next sc, sc in last sc, turn. Rep this row for Seed Stitch.

NOTES

1. The skirt is worked from the lower edge up to lower edge of bodice. The bodice and sleeves are then worked, in one piece, sideways from cuff edge of one sleeve to cuff edge of other sleeve.
2. To change color, work last stitch of old color to last yarn over; yarn over with new color and draw through all loops on hook to complete stitch. Fasten off old color and proceed with new color.

SKIRT (make 2)

With larger hook and A, ch 75 (79, 89, 95, 103).

Row 1 (RS): Sc in 2nd ch from hook, sc in next ch, *ch 1, sk next ch, sc in next ch; rep from * across, turn—74 (78, 88, 94, 102) sts (consisting of 38 (40, 45, 48, 52) sc and 36 (38, 43, 46, 50) ch-1 sps).

Rows 2–6: Work even in Seed Stitch pattern.

Shape Sides

Row 7 (decrease row): Ch 1, sc2tog over first sc and ch-1 sp, *ch 1, sk next sc, sc in next ch-1 sp; rep from * across to last 2 sc, sc2tog over last 2 sc, turn—72 (76, 86, 92, 100) sts.

Rows 8–12: Ch 1, sc in first st, *ch 1, sk next sc, sc in next ch-1 sp; rep from * across to last sc, sc in last sc, turn.

Row 13 (decrease row): Ch 1, sc2tog over first 2 sc, *sc in next ch-1 sp, ch 1, sk next sc; rep from * across to last ch-1 sp, sc2tog over last ch-1 sp and last sc, turn— 70 (74, 84, 90, 98) sts.

Rows 14–18: Work even in Seed Stitch pattern.

Rows 19–42 (42, 54, 54, 66): Rep Rows 7–18, 2 (2, 3, 3, 4) more times—62 (66, 72, 78, 82) sts.

Work even in Seed Stitch pattern until piece measures 8 (9, 9^1/$_2$, 10, 11)"/20.5 (23, 24, 25.5, 28) cm from beginning; end with a RS row and change to B in last st of last row.

Change to smaller hook.

Row 1 (WS): With B, ch 1, sc in first 4 (2, 3, 1, 3) sts, [sc2tog, sc in next 4 (5, 4, 5, 5) sts] 9 (9, 11, 11, 11) times, sc in remaining sts across; change to C in last st, turn— 53 (57, 61, 67, 71) sts.

Rows 2 and 3: With C, ch 1, sc in each sc across, turn.
Fasten off.

Row 4: With RS facing, join B with sl st in first sc, ch 1, sc in first sc, *ldc in next sc 2 rows below, sc in next sc; rep from * across. Fasten off.

Note: Work begins at cuff edge of one sleeve. Work proceeds sideways across bodice, and ends at cuff edge of other sleeve.

With smaller hook and A, ch 32 (36, 42, 42, 44).

Row 1: Dc in 4th ch from hook (beginning ch counts as first dc) and in each ch across, turn— 30 (34, 40, 40, 42) dc.

Row 2: Ch 3 (counts as dc here and throughout), dc in each dc across, turn.

Row 3 (increase row): Ch 3, dc in first dc (increase made), dc in each dc across to last dc (turning ch), 2 dc in last dc (increase made), turn— 32 (36, 42, 42, 44) dc.

Rows 4–7 (7, 7, 9, 11): Rep last 2 rows 2 (2, 2, 3, 4) more times— 36 (40, 46, 48, 52) dc.

Place a stitch marker at the end of the last row for end of the first sleeve shaping.

Row 8 (8, 8, 10, 12): Ch 3, dc in each dc across, turn.

Rep last row until piece measures 5 (6^1/$_2$, 7, 8, 8^1/$_2$)"/12.5 (16.5, 18, 20.5, 21.5) cm from beginning; end with RS row and change to B in last st of last row.

Instructions continued on page 18.

Next 2 Rows: With B, ch 1, sc in each st across, turn. Change to A in last st of last row.

Shape Back Yoke

Row 1: With A, ch 3 (counts as first dc), dc in next 15 (17, 20, 21, 23) sc, turn; leave remaining sts unworked for neck and front yoke—16 (18, 21, 22, 24) sc.

Rows 2–5 (6, 6, 6, 7): Ch 3, dc in each st across, turn. Change to B in last st of last row.

Row 6 (7, 7, 7, 8): With B, ch 1, sc in each st across; change to C in last st, turn.

Row 7 (8, 8, 8, 9) (RS): With C, ch 3, dc in each st across; change to B in last st, turn.

Row 8 (9, 9, 9, 10): With B, ch 1, sc in each st across; change to A in last st, turn.

Rows 9 (10, 10, 10, 11)–12 (14, 14, 14, 16): Ch 3, dc in each st across, turn.
Fasten off.

Shape Front Yoke

Sk 12 (12, 12, 13, 14) unworked sts following back yoke, join A with sl st in next st, ch 3 (counts as dc), dc in each remaining st across—8 (10, 13, 13, 14) dc.

Rows 2–12 (14, 14, 14, 16): Work as for Rows 2–12 (14, 14, 14, 16) of back yoke.
Fasten off.

18

Join Front and Back Yoke

With WS facing, join A in first st at outside edge of last back yoke row.

Joining Row: Ch 3, dc in each st of back yoke across, ch 12 (12, 12, 13, 14) (for neck), dc in each st of last row of front yoke; change to B in last st, turn—36 (40, 46, 48, 52) sts.

Rows 1 and 2: With B, ch 1, sc in each st across, turn. Change to A in last st of last row.

Row 3: With A, ch 3, dc in each st across, turn.

Rep last row until piece measures the same from neck as first half, from neck to stitch marker (at end of shaping of first sleeve).

Next Row (decrease row): Ch 3, dc2tog, dc in each st across to last 3 sts, dc2tog, dc in last st, turn—34 (38, 44, 46, 50) dc.

Next Row: Ch 3, dc in each st across, turn.

Rep last 2 rows 2 (2, 2, 3, 4) more times—30 (34, 40, 40, 42) sts.

Next Row: Ch 3, dc in each st across. Fasten off.

SLEEVE RUFFLE (make 2)

Beginning at lower edge of ruffle, with larger hook and A, ch 39 (43, 51, 51, 55).

Row 1: Sc in 2nd ch from hook, sc in next ch, *ch 1, sk next ch, sc in next ch; rep from * across—38 (42, 50, 50, 54) sts.

Work even in Seed Stitch pattern until piece measures 2 ($2^1/_2$, $2^1/_2$, 3, 3)"/5 (6.5, 6.5, 7.5, 7.5) cm from beginning.

Next Row (decrease row): Ch 1, sc in first 3 (1, 0, 0, 3) sts, [sc2tog, sc in next 2 (3, 3, 3, 2) sts] 8 (8, 10, 10, 12) times, sc in any remaining sts across— 30 (34, 40, 40, 42) sts. Fasten off.

FINISHING

Block pieces to finished measurements. Place two markers along lower edge of front of bodice, one marker $5^1/_4$ ($5^1/_2$, 6, $6^1/_2$, $6^3/_4$)"/ 13.5 (14, 15, 16.5, 17)cm from each side of center front. Sew top edge of one skirt piece between markers. Repeat this process to sew other skirt piece to center back of bodice. Sew side and underarm seams. Sew top of one sleeve ruffle to cuff edge of each sleeve, easing sleeve to fit, and placing opening at center top of sleeve (as shown in photograph).

Neck Edging

With RS facing, join yarn in neck edge at one shoulder, sc evenly around neck edge; join with sl st in first sc. Fasten off.

Embellishment

With yarn needle and B, embroider chain stitches on top of seam line between skirt and bodice, and on top of seam line between sleeve ruffles and sleeves.

Sleeve Bow (make 2)

With smaller hook and B, ch 45. Fasten off. Tie a knot in each end. Tie each piece into a bow and sew one to each sleeve ruffle at top of opening.

Rose

With smaller hook and A, ch 11. Work 3 sc in 2nd ch from hook, 3 sc in next 2 ch, 3 hdc in next 3 ch, 3 dc in next 3 ch, (hdc, sc) in last ch. Fasten off leaving a long tail. Roll piece into a rose shape. Use the tail to sew a few sts into the base of the rose to secure. Sew rose to center front of bodice at neck line.

Using yarn needle, weave in all ends.

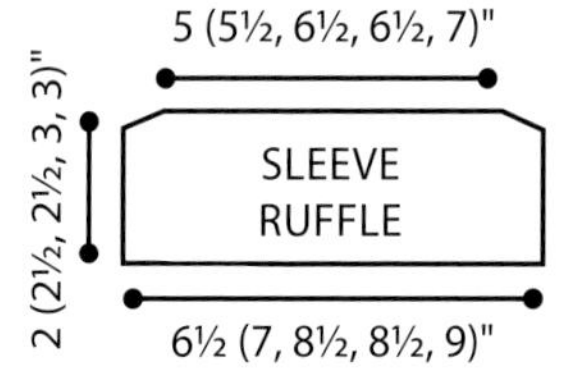

5 (5½, 6½, 6½, 7)"
SLEEVE RUFFLE
2 (2½, 2½, 3, 3)"
6½ (7, 8½, 8½, 9)"

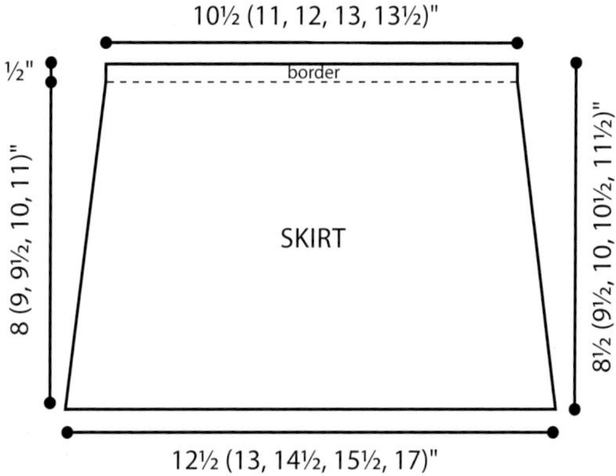

10½ (11, 12, 13, 13½)"
½"
border
SKIRT
8 (9, 9½, 10, 11)"
8½ (9½, 10, 10½, 11½)"
12½ (13, 14½, 15½, 17)"

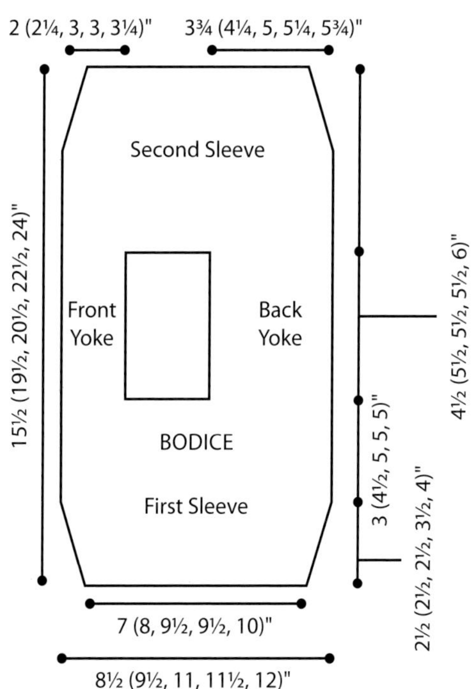

2 (2¼, 3, 3, 3¼)"
3¾ (4¼, 5, 5¼, 5¾)"
Second Sleeve
15½ (19½, 20½, 22½, 24)"
Front Yoke
Back Yoke
4½ (5½, 5½, 5½, 6)"
BODICE
First Sleeve
3 (4½, 5, 5, 5)"
2½ (2½, 2½, 3½, 4)"
7 (8, 9½, 9½, 10)"
8½ (9½, 11, 11½, 12)"

nap time baby
blanket

■■□□ EASY

Shown on page 23.

FINISHED MEASUREMENTS

Width   36"/91.5cm, including border
Length   36"/91.5cm, including border

MATERIALS

Caron International's Naturally Caron Spa
(75% microdenier acrylic, 25% rayon from bamboo;
3 oz/85g, 251 yds/230m):
#0006 Berry Frappe 15 oz (A)
#0003 Soft Sunshine 6 oz (B)
#0002 Coral Lipstick 6 oz (C)

Crochet hook size US F/5 (3.75mm), or size to obtain gauge
Yarn needle

GAUGE

One finished square (including edging) measures about
5 x 5"/12.5 x 12.5 cm.

ABBREVIATIONS

rep   repeat
rnd(s)   round(s)
RS   right side
sk   skip
sp   space
st(s)   stitch(es)
WS   wrong side

SPECIAL TERM

V-st: V-stitch—2 dc in indicated chain or space.

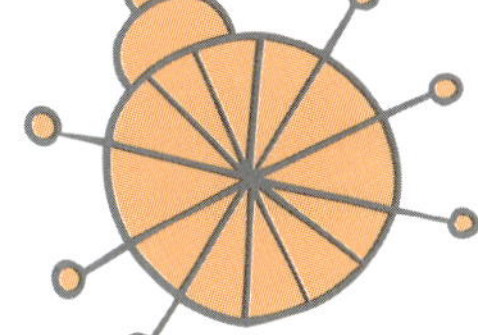

Instructions continued on page 22.

Chain (ch)
Double crochet (dc)
Single crochet (sc)
Slip stitch (sl st)

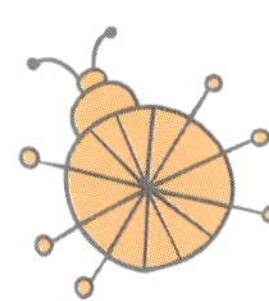

NOTE

To change color, work last stitch of old color to last yarn over; yarn over with new color and draw through all loops on hook to complete stitch. Do not fasten off old color. Carry colors up side of work until needed again. Take care when working edging around striped blocks, to hide carried strands underneath edging stitches.

SOLID BLOCK (make 40 – 16 with A, 12 with B, and 12 with C)
Ch 23.

Row 1 (WS): 2 Dc in 5th ch from hook (V-st made), sk next ch, *V-st in next ch, sk next ch; rep from * across to last ch, dc in last ch, turn—9 V-sts.

Rows 2–12: Ch 3, V-st in sp between 2 dc of each V-st across, dc in top of turning ch, turn.
Fasten off.

Edging

With RS facing, join A in lower corner of block.

Rnd 1: Working across opposite side of foundation ch, work 3 sc in corner, 2 sc at base of each V-st across, and 3 sc in next corner; working up side edge, work 22 sc evenly spaced across edge, 3 sc in corner; working across top edge, work 2 sc in sp between 2 dc of each V-st across, 3 sc in corner; working down remaining side edge, work 22 sc evenly spaced across edge; join with sl st in first sc—92 sc.

Rnd 2: Ch 3, dc in each sc around, working (2 dc, ch 1, 2 dc) in each corner sc (center sc of 3-sc corner); join with sl st in top of beginning ch. Fasten off.

STRIPED BLOCK (make 9)
With B, ch 23.

Row 1 (WS): With B, V-st in 5th ch from hook, sk next ch, *V-st in next ch, sk next ch; rep from * across to last ch, dc in last ch; change to A in last st, turn—9 V-sts.

Row 2: With A, ch 3, V-st in sp between 2 dc of each V-st across, dc in top of turning ch; change to C in last st, turn.

Row 3: With C, ch 3, V-st in sp between 2 dc of each V-st across, dc in top of turning ch; change to B in last st, turn.

Row 4: With B, ch 3, V-st in sp between 2 dc of each V-st across, dc in top of turning ch; change to A in last st, turn.

Rows 5–12: Rep Rows 2–4 two more times, then rep Row 2 and 3 once more.
Fasten off.

Instructions continued on page 24.

| designed by Margret Willson

nap time baby blanket assembly diagram

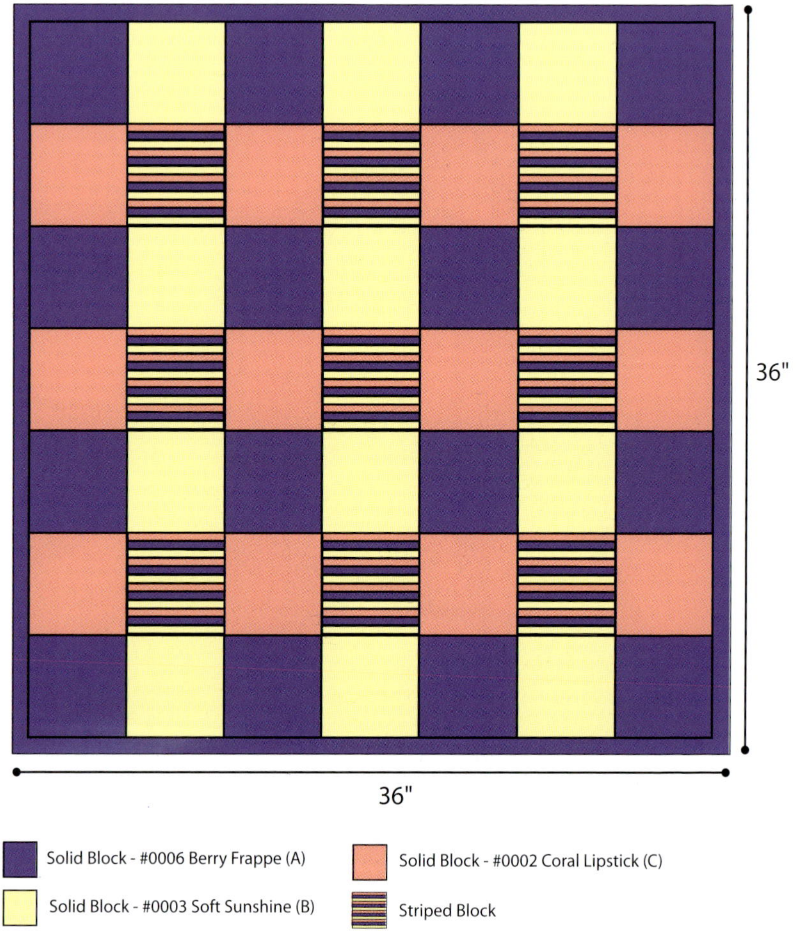
36"
36"
Solid Block - #0006 Berry Frappe (A)
Solid Block - #0003 Soft Sunshine (B)
Solid Block - #0002 Coral Lipstick (C)
Striped Block

Edging

Work same as edging for solid block.

FINISHING

Arrange blocks as shown in assembly diagram. Sl st blocks together as follows: Hold neighboring blocks with WS together and sl st edges together, inserting hook under both loops of edging sts. **Note:** At inside corners, take care to sl st the last block to all 3 previously joined blocks.

Border

Join A in edge of blanket, sc in each dc around, working dc in ch-1 sp of each joined block corner, and 3 sc in each corner of the blanket around; join with sl st in first sc. **Note:** Do not work sc in any of the seams, skip the seams. Fasten off.

Using yarn needle, weave in all ends.

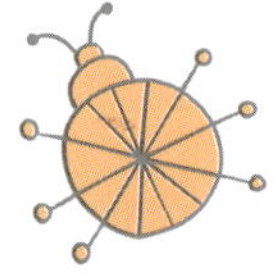

mom's bag

Shown on page 27.

 INTERMEDIATE

FINISHED MEASUREMENTS

Width   12"/30.5cm
Height   10"/25.5cm
Depth   3"/7.5cm

MATERIALS

Caron International's Naturally Caron Spa **LIGHT 3**
(75% microdenier acrylic, 25% rayon from bamboo;
3 oz/85g, 251 yds/230m):
#0004 Green Sheen 12 oz (A)
#0008 Misty Taupe 6 oz (B)
#0007 Naturally 6 oz (C)

Crochet hook size US H/8 (5mm), or size to obtain gauge
Stitch markers
Yarn needle
One button, 1"/25mm diameter or toggle button (for closure)
One buckle, 2"/5cm inside opening measurement (for bag strap)
$^3/_8$yd/0.35m craft felt, 60"/152.5cm wide
Sewing needle and thread (for sewing liner to bag)
Pins

GAUGE

In pattern, 16 sts and 10 rows = 4"/10cm

Instructions continued on page 26.

rep	repeat
rnd(s)	round(s)
RS	right side
sk	skip
st(s)	stitch(es)

SPECIAL TERMS

ldc: Long double crochet—Yarn over, insert hook in indicated st 2 rows below, yarn over and draw up a loop (to current row height), [yarn over and draw through 2 loops on hook] twice. **Note:** Do not work into the corresponding stitch in the current working row.

sc2tog: Single crochet 2 together— Insert hook in next st, yarn over and draw up a loop, (2 loops on hook), insert hook in next st, yarn over and draw up a loop, yarn over and draw through all 3 loops on hook.

STITCHES USED

Chain (ch)
Double crochet (dc)
Single crochet (sc)
Slip stitch (sl st)

NOTES

1. Bag is worked holding two strands of yarn together throughout.
2. To change color, work last stitch of old color to last yarn over; yarn over with new color and draw through all loops on hook to complete stitch. Proceed with new color. When changing color, you can fasten off the old color and rejoin when needed. Alternately, you can carry unused colors up the side of the piece and pick them up when needed. If you choose to carry unused colors, take care that the carried yarns do not become tangled.

COLOR SEQUENCE

Work *2 rows with A, 2 rows with B, 2 rows with C; rep from * as needed.

BAG PANEL (make 3)

Holding 2 strands of A together, ch 50.

Row 1 (RS): Sc in 2nd ch from hook and in each ch across, turn—49 sc.

Row 2: Ch 3 (counts as dc here and throughout), dc in next 2 sts, ch 3, sk next 3 sts, *dc in next 5 sts, ch 3, sk next 3 sts; rep from * across to last 3 sts, dc in last 3 sts; change to 2 strands of B in last st, turn.

Row 3: With B, ch 3, dc in next 2 sts, 3 ldc in center st of 3 skipped sts 2 rows below, *dc in next 5 sts, 3 ldc in center st of 3 skipped sts 2 rows below; rep from * across to last 3 sts, dc in last 3 sts, turn.

Row 4: Ch 3, dc in next 6 sts, *ch 3, sk next 3 sts, dc in next 5 sts; rep from * across to last 2 sts, dc in last 2 sts; change to 2 strands of C in last st, turn.

Row 5: With C, ch 3, dc in next 6 sts, *3 ldc in center st of 3 skipped sts 2 rows below, dc in next 5 sts; rep from * across to last 2 sts, dc in last 2 sts, turn.

Instructions continued on page 28.

| designed by Mary E. Nolfi

Rows 6–25: Continue to change color as in Color Sequence, and rep Rows 2–5 five more times.

Note: The last row is worked with A.

Rows 26 and 27: With A, ch 1, sc in each st across, turn—49 sc. Do not fasten off.

Edging
Rnd 1: With A, ch 1, sc in same st as last sc of Row 27 (top corner made); work 38 sc evenly spaced across side edge, 3 sc in corner; sc in each ch across opposite side of foundation ch, 3 sc in corner; work 38 sc evenly spaced across other side edge; ch 1, sc in same st as first sc of Row 27 (top corner made); join with sl st in first sc. Fasten off. **Note:** You may wish to put a marker in ch-1 sp of each top corner. You will need to know the top of each panel for correct assembly.

GUSSET AND STRAP
Note: One long strip of crochet fabric serves as both gusset and strap. A portion of the gusset/strap will be sewn to two bag panels to form the sides and bottom of the bag.

With 2 strands of A held together, ch 11.

Row 1: Sc in 2nd ch from hook and in each ch across, turn—10 sc.

Rows 2–317: Ch 1, sc in each sc across, turn. Place markers on edges of Row 23.

Rows 318–320: Ch 1, sc2tog, sc in each st across to last 2 sts, sc2tog, turn—4 sc.
Fasten off.

With 2 strands of A held together, join yarn in edge of gusset/strap, work sc evenly around all edges of gusset/strap; join with sl st in first sc. Fasten off leaving a 15"/38cm tail for sewing.

FINISHING
Place bag panels on craft felt and draw around them. Cut out the pieces, cutting about $^1/_4$"/7mm inside the outline. With sewing needle and thread, whipstitch one piece of felt to the WS of each panel, taking care to leave the crochet edges free for crocheting the pieces together.

Cover Buckle (optional)
Place slip knot on hook and take working yarn over top of buckle and hold to the back. *Insert hook, from front to back, through center of buckle and draw up a loop to level of outer edge of buckle, yarn over and draw through both loops on hook to complete a covering sc; rep from * working around the buckle until completely covered with sc. Fasten off.

Assembly

Align marker on Row 23 of gusset/ strap with marker on top of one bag panel (this leaves about 4"/10cm of strap for attaching buckle), arrange one long edge of gusset/strap down side, across bottom, and up opposite side of bag panel, and pin edges of gusset/strap and panel together (remainder of gusset/strap serves as the strap). With 2 strands of A held together, WS of pieces together, and working through both thicknesses, sc evenly around to join edge of gusset to edge of bag panel. Fasten off.

Add buckle and lining to gusset/ strap: After the gusset/strap is attached to one bag panel, thread buckle onto straight end of gusset/ strap, fold over about 1"/2.5cm of strap, and sew in place on WS to secure buckle. Cut piece of craft felt to line the gusset. Cut the felt to extend from the buckle fold, along the inside of the bag, to the opposite top edge of the panel, leave strap portion of gusset/strap unlined. Sew liner in place along gusset/strap. Cut liner for curved end of strap about 8"/20.5cm long, and sew in place.

Join second bag panel to opposite long edge of gusset/strap in same manner as first bag panel. With crochet hook, pull all yarn ends between liners and crochet panels.

Hold RS of third panel and one panel of assembled bag (this will be the back of the bag) together. Working from inside top of bag, with 2 strands of A held together and working through both thicknesses, join yarn in top corner, work sc evenly across to center of top edge, ch 15, sc in 14th and 15th ch from hook to form a loop, ch 1 and sl st in each ch around the loop, work sc evenly across top edge to opposite top corner. Fasten off.

Thread curved end of strap through buckle and adjust to desired length. Sew button to center top of front of bag.

Using yarn needle, weave in all ends.

sweet dreams
baby blanket

 **EASY**

FINISHED MEASUREMENTS
Width 32"/81.5cm, straight edge to straight edge

MATERIALS
Caron International's Naturally Caron Spa **LIGHT 3**
(75% microdenier acrylic, 25% rayon from bamboo;
3 oz/85g, 251 yds/230m):
#0004 Green Sheen 6 oz (A)
#0007 Naturally 6 oz (B)
#0005 Ocean Spray 6 oz (C)

Crochet hook size US G/6 (4mm), or size to obtain gauge
Yarn needle

GAUGE
Rnds 1–3 measure approximately 4$^{1}/_{4}$"/10.75cm at widest point;
In pattern, 6 pattern repeats (6 clusters and 5 spaces) and
8 rows = 4"/10cm.

ABBREVIATIONS
rep	repeat
rnd(s)	round(s)
RS	right side
sp(s)	space(s)

SPECIAL TERMS
Beg-Cl: Beginning Cluster—Ch 3, yarn over, insert hook in indicated
sp and draw up a loop; yarn over and draw through 2 loops on hook,
[yarn over, insert hook in same sp and draw up a loop; yarn over and
draw through 2 loops on hook] twice, yarn over and draw through all
4 loops on hook.

Instructions continued on page 32.

| designed by Karen Drouin

Cl: Cluster—Yarn over, insert hook in indicated sp and draw up a loop; yarn over and draw through 2 loops on hook, [yarn over, insert hook in same sp and draw up a loop; yarn over and draw through 2 loops on hook] 3 times, yarn over and draw through all 5 loops on hook.

STITCHES USED
Chain (ch)
Double crochet (dc)
Half double crochet (hdc)
Single crochet (sc)
Slip stitch (sl st)

NOTE
Blanket is worked in joined rounds, with RS facing throughout.

COLOR SEQUENCE
Work 2 rnds with A, 1 rnd with B, 2 rnds with C, [1 rnd with B, 2 rnds with A, 1 rnd with B, 2 rnds with C] 4 times.

BLANKET
With A, ch 4; join with sl st in first ch to form a ring.

Rnd 1 (RS): Beg-Cl in ring, [ch 3, Cl in ring] 5 times; join with ch 1, hdc in beg-Cl (join counts as ch-3 sp here and throughout)—6 clusters, and 6 ch-3 sps.

Rnd 2: Beg-Cl in first ch-sp (formed by join), [ch 3, (Cl, ch 3, Cl) in next ch-3 sp] 5 times, ch 3, Cl in same ch-sp as beg-Cl; join with ch 1, hdc in beg-Cl—12 clusters, and 12 ch-3 sps. Fasten off.

Rnd 3: Join B with sl st in joining ch-sp, beg-Cl in same ch-sp, ch 3, (Cl, ch 3, Cl) in next ch-3 sp (corner made), *ch 3, Cl in next ch-3 sp, ch 3, (Cl, ch 3, Cl) in next ch-3 sp (corner made); rep from * around; join with ch 1, hdc in beg-Cl—18 clusters, and 18 ch-3 sps. Fasten off.

Rnd 4: Join C with sl st in any corner ch-3 sp, beg-Cl in same ch-sp, [ch 3, Cl in next ch-3 sp] to next corner ch-3 sp, *ch 3, (Cl, ch 3, Cl) in corner ch-3 sp, [ch 3, Cl in next ch-3 sp] to next corner ch-3 sp; rep from * around, ch 3, Cl in same ch-sp as beg-Cl; join with ch 1, hdc in beg-Cl—24 clusters, and 24 ch-3 sps.

Rnds 5–29: Continue to change color as in Color Sequence and rep Rnd 4 until a total of 29 rnds have been worked. **Notes:** 1) When 2 rnds of the same color are worked, you do not have to fasten off and rejoin the yarn between the first and 2nd rnd. 2) The last rnd will be worked with C and will have 174 clusters, and 174 ch-3 sps.

FINISHING
Border
With RS facing, join B in any ch-3 sp. Rnd 1: Ch 1, (sc, hdc, dc, hdc, sc) in each ch-3 sp around; join with sl st in first sc. Fasten off.

Using yarn needle, weave in all ends.